"Peter Stiles' poems deepen the insights of all who read C. S. Lewis and will help a new generation to turn to Lewis as a guide in faith's journey. Peter's poems explore that brilliant mind that came alive via conversion to a Christian faith informed by the best university scholarship in philosophy and literature, and in his vocation to write, speak and live the faith. Stiles catches Lewis' capacity for friendship, for love and for the lived experience of suffering and loss.

Stiles' personal approach to Lewis via poetry is a gift to the reader. Stiles himself exhibits a commitment to close and minute observation and to an inner awareness that lines up with the poetic moment. All his poems risk a personal edge and some deeply so. *Coming Home, Sehnsucht [longing]*, and *The Equestrian Accident* are three poems of particular dignity, strength, core insight and narrative moment.

Each in its own way catches a central theme found in Lewis' work. They, and the volume, add to that weight of glory which Lewis was touched by, and sought, and expressed brilliantly in his war time address of the same name."

– REV DR IVAN HEAD
was Warden of two Australian University Colleges

"Unlike Tolkien, who is marvellously monolithic, there are many points of entry into the work of that other giant, C. S. Lewis; and that gives us reason to rejoice here. In *Surprised by Jack*, Peter Stiles takes us back into his life and work, lived and shared. That experience brought me a quiet, heartfelt joy, as did the later poems about his wife and family. A great read."

– DR DAVID CRAIG
Professor of English, Franciscan University of Steubenville, Ohio

"These lovingly crafted poems are about people and places, memories and emotions, and the art of poetry which understands the importance of the well-loved pen from which words and metaphors flow. They are also deeply Christian, though never intrusively so. Many of them grow from the experience of reading the books of C. S. Lewis or engaging with his life in Belfast, in Oxford or the mythical lands that began in his fertile imagination. Others are rooted in the Blue Mountains near Sydney, reminding readers from the northern hemisphere that the seasons are reversed, but the birds and the trees, though exotic, are still familiar. Peter Stiles has a beautifully deft and gentle way with words and rhythms, his poems catching moments and memories – places in time."

– THE REV CANON PROFESSOR DAVID JASPER
DD FRSE, *Emeritus Professor – University of Glasgow*
Honorary Professorial Research Fellow

"The verse of Peter Stiles is like the man himself – gentle, insightful, and full of a wisdom that lingers in your mind for months and years to come. These poems beautifully interweave the life and thinking of C. S. Lewis, Peter's own experience of suffering and beauty, and the subtle influence of the mountain home to which he loves to retreat. Engaging with these words enables the reader to experience life afresh – with a renewed vision, awake to all the splendour and mystery of life."

– DR MARK STEPHENS, *Lecturer in New Testament,*
Sydney Missionary and Bible College; Research Fellow,
Centre for Public Christianity

"Most words communicate but few retain their colour after sunset. In the poetry of Peter Stiles, words are gifted to the reader, and in this collection, the life and work of C. S. 'Jack' Lewis lends its hue and colour to each precious gift of word or phrase from the pen of Stiles. In this collection, Stiles crafts his gifts lovingly, and thoughtfully, to leave us alone with Lewis. Sitting in his company, the words of Lewis read and surprise us, as surely as do the words of Stiles. Their words are gifted to the reader in the anticipation that they will evoke impressions and memories. So, the Malvern Hills, Narnia, Lewis, and perhaps even Stiles himself, become more real to us. Though for Lewis, the Oxford sun finally set in 1963, the poetry of Peter Stiles shines an evening light that is as hopeful as it is colourful."

– REV ASSOCIATE PROFESSOR DARRELL JACKSON,
Whitley College, University of Divinity

NOTE:
Cover image is of 'The Kilns',
C.S. Lewis' home in Oxford,
taken by 'jschroe' from Kailua-Kona, Hawaii.

Surprised by Jack
a poetic response to C.S. Lewis

&

A Handful of Quietness
poems inspired by The Blue Mountains

by

Peter Stiles

ISBN: 978-0-6484451-2-8

© 2022

Published by **Poetica Christi Press**
42 Hawkins Rd, Montrose, 3765
Email : poetica@iprimus.com.au
Website : www.poeticachristi.org.au

Cover design and book layout by:
Wattle and Willow Books
www.facebook.com/wattleandwillowbooks

The cover photo of 'The Kilns' is
taken by 'jschroe' from Kailua-Kona, Hawaii,
and has been sourced from Wikimedia Commons
and used under their Creative Common Licence.

Copyright for this book belongs to **Peter Stiles**.
Reproduction of poems from this book is allowable for
non-commercial use only but acknowledgement
of authorship is required.

To Kerrie,
my always loving and supportive wife.
Her nourishing presence in my life
gives me energy, creativity,
faith and hope.

Contents

Surprised by Jack

Introduction	12
The Hospital café	14
Phantastes	16
Boxton	17
The Kilns	18
Jack at Macquarie Hospital	19
The Weight of Glory	20
The Eagle and Child	21
Durham Cathedral	22
The Malvern Hills	23
Letters to an American Lady	24
Passing	25
The First Edition	26
Malacandra	27
Perelandra	28
Words Are Slow	29
'the singing of a lark'	30
Sehnsucht	31
The Equestrian Accident	32
Coming Home	33
Morning Light	34
Pentecost Sunday	35
Le Lion et la Sorcière Blanche	36
Ichthus	38
The Scholar	39
The Father's House	40

Jack at Wentworth Falls	41
Friendship	42
Longing	43
A Grief Observed	44

In the Blue Mountains

Lent in the Blue Mountains	49
Silence	50
Mountain Mist	51
Trinity Sunday, Wentworth Falls	52
The Bird Call	53
The Golden Mile	54
Fire on the Mountain	55
A Handful of Quietness	56
The Lone Wolf	57
Bird Life	58
Lamplight	59
The Crown of Thorns	60
The Waterman Pen	62
Metaphors	63
My Wife	64
Resignation	65
Acknowledgements	66
About The Author	67

Surprised by Jack

a poetic response to C.S. Lewis

Introduction

For many years C.S. Lewis dwelt on the fringes of my devotional reading and academic interests. I had always respected and admired him and his writings, but had not had the opportunity to respond as I would have liked. But in the summer of 2015, during a seven week stay in Oxford, I heard Walter Hooper, the Lewis aficionado, interviewed about his life's commitment twice, in two lengthy interviews for American Christian television. I also visited The Kilns for the first time. For whatever reason, I suddenly saw Lewis' life and writings with fresh eyes and enthusiasm, an appreciation greatly enhanced by reading Alister McGrath's fine biography, *C. S. Lewis – A Life* (amongst others), and re-reading many of Lewis' works of varying genres in subsequent months.

Jack Lewis was an intriguing man. A very gifted intellectual and teacher, a prolific author, a vibrant and jovial companion, a compassionate, dutiful correspondent, and a devoted family man, he lived a life that unquestionably exhibited the transformative nature of a life given over to serving Jesus Christ. Lewis recognised his literary gifts, his developed gifts as a communicator generally, and he used them deliberately, effectively and extensively for the glory of God.

It is difficult to detach the man from his literary output. His domestic life, his years as a Don, first at Oxford, and then later, Cambridge, and the corpus of his literary output, have all generated an intense amount of interest from scholars and general readers around the world. So, in compiling this collection of my poems about him, I have interleaved verse concerning the vast breadth of his impressive literary collection of writings with aspects of his daily life in Oxford and elsewhere.

Several of the poems represent specific, quite moving responses that came from particular readings, as I have kept company with this great man in recent years. It has been a rich, rewarding experience.

For readers unfamiliar with the life and work of Lewis, here are some brief biographical details. Charles Staples Lewis (1898-1963) grew up in Northern Ireland, on the outskirts of Belfast. He was educated at several schools, and just prior to going up to Oxford, had a very influential personal tutor, William Kirkpatrick. Both he and his elder brother, Warren (or Warnie as he was known) lived through two world wars, both serving in different capacities. Over time, Jack Lewis established himself as an outstanding scholar and lecturer, having gained a triple First at Oxford and going on to become a Fellow and Tutor at Magdalen College.

In 1929 Lewis became a committed Christian, and subsequently established himself as one of the foremost Christian writers of the twentieth century. He was an excellent linguist and throughout his life maintained a keen interest in Norse mythology. In Oxford, he lived at The Kilns, a beautiful old home in Headington, Oxford. It is now a study centre for Lewis scholars. In 1954 Lewis became Professor of Mediaeval and Renaissance Literature at Cambridge University. In 1956 he married Joy Davidman, an intellectually gifted American divorcee. It was a very happy marriage, but cancer took her life four years later. Lewis died in 1963, on the same day that President J.F. Kennedy was assassinated. Lewis has left behind a diverse and rewarding legacy of publications for readers today.

— PETER STILES

The Hospital Cafe

I always choose the same table. Blocked on one side by a central pillar, it faces out onto a sunny, paved courtyard, where people pass on their way into the hospital or to the university lecture theatres nearby. It is easy to distinguish between the students, the sober visitors and the well-dressed doctors purposefully striding to their appointments. A pot of tea and a lemon slice are enough to sustain for the period of time my wife is undergoing radiotherapy in rooms beneath me. I settle down to write. It is noisy. People at tables chatter animatedly, while others sit alone, waiting, staring into some void of uncertainty regarding the condition of someone they love. It is an ever-changing scene.

I turn my attention to my writing. At first the words come slowly. Then, as an idea forms, the images emerge and come together, a creative impulse towards poetic expression. The voices in the background are dulled by concentration, now no more noticeable than air conditioning. I am 'in the zone'. Time evaporates. I keep on writing, wrestling with the best words, inverting, substituting, clarifying, finessing. I am absorbed by the process, sunshine pouring onto the crazed pine tabletop. The page becomes a spider's web of words, some crossed out, others slotted in above the line, some in the margins. I read over what I have written, listening for rhythm, for assonance, for an emerging form. I hear the poem like a song in my mind. It longs to be sung.

I look up. Last time, I noticed at the table opposite, a young doctor with pre-Raphaelite features comparing notes with her older male colleague. She hung on every word he said, her eyes sparkling with intelligent inquiry. They are gone, and now there is a poised, African woman, stylishly dressed, staring at her laptop. She pensively sips from her coffee cup.

I plunge back into the poem, polishing it, rounding corners, cutting out the dead word, the redundant image. I arrange the lines with care, as you would the pieces of a puzzle. Then, eventually, comes a sense of completeness, as I read over the poem again and again, tweaking commas, sensing its wholeness. I pause. Something has gone out of me, an ineffable feeling that almost catches my breath. I believe. Lifting my head, I smile at those around me. The chatter and the cacophony of crockery sounds continue.

Phantastes

Leatherhead Station in October,
   and stillness on the long, deserted station.
Waiting, a young man gazes over
     distant hills beyond the Dorking Valley,
        intensely blue in the frosty, evening light.
The clarity of cold, autumnal air,
   gratifying lucidity.
Fading day, the standing locomotive's glow,
   familiar, calming smoke of a steam engine.
Buoyed by the promise of a weekend,
    he turns to the bookstall,
       the dust-soiled MacDonald novel
      catching his eye.
This is a point-changing moment,
  a lever shift to remember for decades.
The Saxon voice of the porter calls
   Bookham, Effingham, Horsley,
     and then beyond, and then beyond.

Note: a significant incident from *Surprised by Joy*.

Boxton

He came into this world creating worlds,
   piecing together things that he soon gleaned,
     figures, spaces, rules of feeling.
He played at the edges of a mythic gleam,
   men and animals, soldiers, kings,
     borders and conquests in his nascent dream.
There was safety in this childhood realm,
   loss that was shared, righted grief,
     a cartoonist sketching a fallen figure
       back into a picture frame.
Returning from school, back to his books,
   within the orbit of his father's care,
     a place of stillness, if chill reserve,
       his mother's hairbrush on the sill.
There he spent his summer days.
Sometimes,
   Warnie laughing down the hall.
But always, at night,
   sighing in the distance, Belfast.
A call into the plainer world of pain.

The Kilns

I have been here before.
From the moment we parked outside, I knew it.
There is Jack, out in the morning light,
    greeting the gardener, Fred, his 'indispensable factotum',
        his deep voice donning the streets of Headington.
The air is still, with August warmth,
   the path to the front door crested with climbing roses.
The latch lifts.
From inside, through a familiar window,
   Jack and Joy still lean against that garden wall.
The blackout curtains are there yet,
    a reminder of dark nights, and lightless train trips to London,
       steaming through, like pot after pot of steeped ideas,
          ready for those famous BBC radio talks.
This is the desk he works at. Touch it.
In sepia tones he sits there,
   paper, pen, Quink ink, tin of tobacco, pipe,
      crafting Christological concepts,
         answering a shuffle of letters with equal care.
In the shadows a household of voices,
    Warnie, Minto, evacuee Jill,
       attendant tones through the tangle of years.
Outside, I tip my hat to the cat before
   we head back down the streets he knows,
     into the bustling mind of Oxford.

Jack at Macquarie Hospital

As I sit here, waiting for my wife each day,
    I think about you, Jack.
I read your words, consider your thoughts,
    foster your life in the distant streets of Oxford.
In the chatter of this busy cafe,
    I hear your sonorous voice,
        sense your smile, the lightness of your step.
Concentrating,
        this place becomes The Trout, and
            you are seated opposite,
                swaddling the air with pipe smoke,
                    a pint of lager before you.
Today you tell me of Norse mythology,
        your eyes bright as you connect the strands
            that weave our salvific story.
As you knock out your pipe, Jack,
    I am warm with satisfaction.

The Weight of Glory

A summer evening in June,
    light lingering in the Oxford sky.
Freshly streaked with tracers,
    and the bass clef growl of bombers,
        it is still tonight,
            listening for the soft timbre of his voice.
A crowded church – weary, war-worn faces,
    drinking words of gossamer, not gore,
        of what awaits the believing heart.
In the back pew, an undergraduate stirs,
    pinning salvation to his chest.
Tomorrow he leaves for the battle ranks.

Note: after 'The Weight of Glory', a sermon that C.S. Lewis delivered during Solemn Evensong at Oxford University Church of St. Mary the Virgin, 8th June, 1941.

The Eagle and Child

This pub, set quietly in the bustle of Oxford,
    near to bus stop throngs, rebutting careful scrutiny,
        for me is draped in bunting, bright,
            a space that snatches thought and awe.

Through the seasons tourists pour
    for food and drinks though this narrow door.
My appetite to render vivid the moments
    when the Inklings drank and laughed and read,
        to savour the flow of their weekly thread.

I can see the seats, they are empty now,
    but wisdom, erudition, wit,
        have been etched into the worn woodwork.
If only this wood became paper, then pages,
    the Bird and Babe would sing for these sages.

Durham Cathedral

How many days I walked those streets
   not knowing you had been before.
The beauty of this Norman splendour
   perfectly poised on a river bend,
     gracing my walls in etchings and prints,
       indelible in my understanding.
I imagine the audience for your lectures,
   the coal-black comfort of your erudition,
     'a little oasis in the dreariness of war',
       three days with Warnie away from the wastage.
The year before a 'Cuthbert cloud'
   protected this jewel from Luftwaffe lust,
     that you might walk in its vaulted splendour,
       that I may glimpse from Palace Green
         the lessons of God's faithfulness.

The three Riddell Memorial Lectures, sponsored by the University of Durham, were given over three days by C. S. Lewis in February, 1943. Warnie accompanied Lewis on the trip to Durham. The lectures became the basis for *The Abolition of Man*.

The Malvern Hills

Lewis loved the Malvern Hills.
From their green spine the shires
    spread like a brushstroke before him.
I have the photos,
    and Elgar alludes to the delighting music
        of their summer evenings.

But, as with Narnia, I have never been there.

Trusting their reality, I press on,
    sharing his taste for the more
        tangible delights of marmalade and tea.

Letters to an American lady

As a fletcher fashions feathers for careful flight,
    his measured letters gave her the spur
        to press on with a vexed life journey.
Balancing wisdom on many issues,
    health, scripture, friendships and family fissures,
        his fountain pen flowed over many years.
From Magdalen, The Kilns, or Cambridge halls,
    he faithfully penned in a close, cramped hand
        to a distant woman in a foreign land.
Crafted in the dewy, cobwebby hours,
    his volume of faith-filled letters now
        sits on my bookshelf,
            a testament to truth and fellowship.

Passing

I remember well the day you died.
  In my quiet New England home
    to be shocked awake
      by news of the other death
        that seized the airwaves of the world.
Back from college,
  my mother standing at the door,
    slicing my slumber with her voice alarmed,
      the morning light from High Street
        drenching panelled walls and fireplace.
That day your passing went unnoticed.
Far from me then the life that kindles kinship,
  awe, a fulcrum on my journey.
But now I see that day for all its worth.

The First Edition

You gave me a first edition of Christian Behaviour.
  It sits comfortably on the bookshelf,
    dressed in its worn dust jacket,
      amidst other modern editions of his work,
        their vibrant, glossy covers distracting the eye.
Making no overt claims,
  like an ancient abbey aware of its history,
    this first edition draws me closer
      to the writing hand,
        the manuscript on the table,
          the ink barely dry.
I cannot recover that moment, but,
  like a war-weary Oxford believer,
    I imagine this new release in Blackwell's window.

Malacandra

(a planet visited by Ransom in *Out of the Silent Planet*)

Worlds we do not know are hard to love.
Distrustful thoughts invade our willing minds.
Until we see the colours and the contours
   – fresh distillations that surprise the eye,
     we assume mundane or fearful prospects.
We are needing to be willed into wonder,
   called away from patterned perception,
     eyes opened to an unseen spectrum.
Distances, shades, perspectives
   that quicken our thinking,
     that let us smile with seasoned breathing.

The air so fresh with sweetened traces,
   a new morning on a verdant mountain,
     with trees as tall as human cathedrals.
By streams of cut diamond purity,
   we glimpse the Eilidil in the rockspray.
Meldilorn.
The pale red hues of peaceful Meldilorn,
   a city of creatures becalmed by care.
Sorns, hrossa, pfifltriggi,
   strange by name but not by nature,
     Oyarsa obedient citizens.
The chosen can stay here and rest in safety.

Perelandra

*(another planet visited by Ransom and the title
of the second book of Lewis' space trilogy)*

Our lives are like a floating world,
    cresting and plunging into seas unknown.
We grasp, like Ransom, at some certainty,
    some green solidity, some terra firma.
Today's news is tomorrow's memory.
Sea currents of concern so quickly fade,
    shoals of sand and shallows
        flooded by foam-flecked zones of time.
We struggle for balance, for a sound footing,
   our torn meniscus aching with unsteadiness,
    a virtual realm of vertigo,
      sweeping us into chasms of doubt,
        puzzlement, deceptive banks of seaweed,
      where, drenched with life,
        we rest to draw our salty breath.
Sometimes there are spots on the horizon,
   just visible behind the surging waves,
    a colour, a flag, a beacon, a call,
      the murmur of some otherness.
Then down again into the murky depths,
    the churn of waterpower in our ears,
      before ascending on a surge of hope,
        glancing again to the dim horizon.

Words Are Slow

(after a line from *Perelandra*)

Words are slow,
    as Ransom found, describing Perelandra.
Threading together words takes time,
    a patterning of lines and dyes
        from which a clear-edged form emerges.
A feeling, concept, idea, whim,
    clear in the mind, is clearer still
        when wrapped in deftly textured words
            that flow through the fabric seamlessly,
                catching the breath in vivid cohesion.
Painstakingly woven in splendid display,
    words release and render meaning,
        a coronation robe for consideration.

'... there came to me in the fresh stillness the singing of a lark'

(a line from *The Great Divorce*)

A pristine morning's stillness, and,
   the clear call of arrival;
      a lark's familiar lyrics.

Here I can rest.

The rocking motion of the bus,
   the hard seats, the blurred landscape
      are now just a memory.

Before me a river of aqua-gold,
   an emblem from a story told,
      a book I have read from childhood.

If I close my eyes I can see
   backwards, honeysuckle brocading
      my earliest years.

From this riverbank
   a fishnet of memories,
      an interleaving of pain and peace.

This was my life.

I have always bought return tickets,
   but not this time.

Sehnsucht*

In our garden is a place,
   known with affection as Goethe's rock.
Decades ago in Heidelberg,
   we gazed down over town and torrent
      from where he sat, from where he walked,
         from where he crafted his deepest lines.
But beauty and desire fade,
   the colours dull, the dyes not fast –
      his thoughts are more elusive now.

We long to see where we cannot be,
   to be in a realm that we only glimpse,
      the moment that brought another to tears,
         the cleft that revealed some otherness.
Daily our eyes crave for somewhere else,
   a space that we have never seen,
      except in mirrored images,
         through Mendelssohn or other means.

Seamlessly the Neckar flows,
   the glimpses that we have suffice.
      We wait for that other world to be revealed.

---

* Sehnsucht : a German word meaning yearning or longing, a condition C. S. Lewis considers in *Surprised by Joy*.

The Equestrian Accident

(with reference to *Miracles*, Chapter 16)

She was only nineteen,
   softly spoken, her eyes spangling.
At a routine jump, clipping the bar,
   her horse fell, killing her instantly.
The field was clutched with sadness.

In another place, greater mounts,
  winged and shining,
     snort and paw the air in expectation.
There is excitement in the King's stables.

Coming Home

(after reading the early chapters of *Surprised by Joy*)

Coming home from college on that slow New England train,
   steaming through a eucalyptic haze,
      the expectation of parental warmth, the open fire's glow,
      sleeping in the country cottage stillness.
The days to talk, to read, to walk,
   the Dietrich Fischer-Dieskau balm
      of turntabling Schubert Lieder.
These are the days I recall so well,
   and even more the promise and the spell.

Morning Light

Leave me alone with Lewis.
He gifts May mornings with sunshine,
   as I sit here in another hospital cafe.
As I copy his ideal day,
    reading and writing in these matin moments,
       I glean the peace that only his presence proffers,
          his words, his phrases jostling in my mind.

By reading his work, he reads me,
    setting antipodean angst in calm perspective,
       like a curator knowing how to place a canvas.

He reads my childhood desires, my solitary hours,
   with the local library then my best, true friend.
He reads my love of God, the Whipsnade ride
   that turned his life about,
     and also opened, early, my ark of treasures.
He reads my lexical longings,
   piecing together letters, crafting meaning,
     the pleasure of a sign and single sentence.

Mornings like this define my diary,
   circled in red and asterisked for emphasis.

Pentecost Sunday

(after a line from The Weight of Glory)

A warm afternoon in May.
We planted leptospermum bushes
   in the fading light,
      bathing in the beauty of this finest foliage,
         mistings of green
            set into the fresh soil.
Gloves, spade and mattock,
   we laboured to release their
      witness to another day beyond, where we become
         what here we only see.
But this scene is bounty enough for today.

Le Lion et la Sorcière Blanche*

Morning light in Paris.
In the garden two children read
   of a wardrobe that leads to another world,
     a place of magic and mystery.
Their world, fractured,
   but free at last, now they can linger in childhood dreams
     of a lion that can conquer all evil schemes
       with safety and comfort and love.

* The first of the *Narnia* series, *The Lion, the Witch and the Wardrobe.* was published in French under this title in 1952.

Le Lion et la Sorcière Blanche

A Paris dans la lumière du matin.
Où lisent deux enfants au jardin
    d'une armoire qui mène à un autre monde,
        un lieu magique et mystérieux.
Leur monde, cassé, mais libre enfin,
    à présent ils restent dans les rêves de l'enfance
        d'un lion, le vainqueur des projets malfaisants
           avec l'amour légendaire et le confort.

Note: translated together-with my wife, Kerrie.

Ichthus

No net less wide than a man's whole heart,
no less fine mesh of love, will hold the
sacred Fish. (from *Reflections on the Psalms*)

Breakfast. Steeping tea and toast.
The gas fire breaks the morning chill,
   aglow in the less lit room.

In our prayers,
    we cast a net into the day,
       seeking your glistening presence,
       clutching to your truths.

We prayed for a finer mesh of love,
    binding strands of unworthy thread
    into a place where you might rest,
    nestled beneath this netting.

Come close, sacred Fish,
   graffiti our grateful hearts
     with Ichthus at every turning.

Let our net almost break
   with the bounty of your loving.

Adonai.

The Scholar

After an interview with Walter Hooper

A young man when you first met Jack,
   now fifty years of keeping him before you,
      constantly reviewing his variegated canvas.
For you the understated scholar's life –
   searching, scanning, sorting,
      fostering a love that grew from first encounters,
         when you drank tea and more tea at The Kilns.

Elderly now,
   the light of those first memories colours thoughts,
      talking of the few months that you shared.
When Jack was gone,
   you took the brush strokes of a great mind,
      and drew together his palette of manuscripts,
         tidying up the remnants of a life poured out in words.
You collected, arranged and built his reputation,
   a role accepted in humility,
      that the many hues of C. S. Lewis may be seen.

The Father's House

Some also have wished that the next way to their Father's house were here that they might be troubled no more with either Hills or Mountains to go over; but the way is the way and there's an end.
(John Bunyan, as quoted in *The Pilgrim's Regress*)

Sometimes that place seemed right –
  familiar sounds, familiar smells,
    the same light seeping through the curtains.
I had a father once,
  who quietly whistled in the next room.
At home with his comfort, I needed little else,
  my days always circling homeward,
    like a kestrel drawn to a falconer.

Those years have passed.

Now I am drawn over many hills and mountains,
  this Father near, but also far,
    calling me to a place beyond these valleys,
      through the tangle of this bracken,
        shadowed clefts, a glimpse of light,
          to the Father's house I long for.

The gravity of His grace propels me.

Jack at Wentworth Falls

Darwin walked here, so why couldn't you,
   you would have liked the silence too,
      the attention to glory in these cliffs,
         the lustre of eucalypt leaves underfoot.
A turn in the track, a smooth rock shelf,
   a place to pause for a ploughman's lunch.
The sun is high, so an hour now
   to read, or write, or muse and pray,
      to give some centre to this day.
Other walkers pass, you smile and wave,
   sensing their whispers and startled glances;
      'That's Dr. Lewis, the Oxford Don,
         famous for faith and his literature classes'.

Friendship

(In response to reading a letter by C.S. Lewis, in Latin, to Don Giovanni Calabria, in January, 1949.)

We live within the compass of
   the mountains and the seas
      that circumscribe our seasons.
The slender thread of Latin linked you to this saint,
   your common code of love
      a twining of voices for
         this ragged garment of humanity.
Casting words upon the page like seeds,
   searching for a deeper soil than dogma,
      your friendship flourished.
You shall meet in a place beyond our telling,
   where Latin lyrics sing,
      where soaring bell towers ring.

Longing

*Do you remember? The colour and the smell, and
looking across at the Grey Mountain in the distance?
And because it was so beautiful, it set me longing,
always longing. Somewhere else there must be
more of it.* – Psyche, in *Till We Have Faces*

A mountain grey, with gilded edges,
   distant, yet dazing in the evening light.
An aim, a goal, a verdant venture,
   a fading moment, this sighting, craving.
In the crowded streets remember the brightening,
   the splendid otherness beyond,
      a position, a promise, a knowing gesture,
         a trace for faith, a scoping of ridges.
Searching this delicate diorama,
   these glistening origami peaks,
      like Psyche we await another.

A Grief Observed

I observed your grief,
   these sittings of confusion,
      pain and emptiness.
Lost in a library of feelings,
   you clutched at words of recovery
      of hope, a knock, a whisper,
         that this is a mistake,
           tomorrow different.
The balm of belief is better than none,
   but words drop into outer space,
      a place where language has no answers,
      a clueless crossword puzzle.
Terrifying terra, without firma,
   an abstraction that lacks explanation,
      a canvas that cannot be placed.
You write of what I know.
The rawness of your words reads mine.
Death is the strangest mystery.

A Handful of Quietness

poems inspired by The Blue Mountains

Lent in the Blue Mountains

Every day now
   the lengthening shadow lines of Lent.
The trees here are tinged with amber,
   silence their best companion.
We are entering a winsome world,
   where, a russet sadness renders every scene,
     coolness clings to every plan
       and timber is stacked
         beside the house for wood fires.

In the evenings we draw a blanket up,
   and read into the darkening hours,
     conscious of the journey that is coming.

Every year we map these shortening days,
   this bruised beauty before our hearts,
     strolling through quiet streets ablaze
       with the colours of grace,
         banners for a life that banished death.

Silence

Here the sough of silence washes over me,
   the stillness of Sunday morning in these trees.
The moment when we draw back into life,
   folding the past and present into one.
Like ointment on the eczema of our limbs,
   this is a soothing place, a calming trope,
     a safe place to inhabit in our thoughts.
There are pools of words that surface in this silence,
   charms that spill out glinting in the sun.
Memories from childhood are most common
   and memories from when our children laughed,
     for them the sheer delight of living.
Silence is nourishing, a prayer,
   these trees, long-standing witnesses to silence,
     whisper in accord.

Mountain Mist

An hour after the hailstorm
  the mist closed in,
    bandaging the white, bruised landscape.
As we walked down the street
  it swept in clouds towards us,
    pinpoints of moisture on my summer shirt.
Cool and sweet after the summer heat,
  it dissolved the focus of February,
    blurring the outline of every picket fence.
The streetlights came on.
This was now a different world,
  ethereal and peaceful.
No bird called, no child cried,
  just the stillness of relief;
    a window into contentment,
      this Wunderkind of kindness.

Trinity Sunday, Wentworth Falls

1.

Silence. Evening. The rain has stopped.
My mind arcs to many places
   like route maps in a glossy airline magazine.
But stillness, not motion, is the central motif here,
   mountains of dark trees
      knit tightly into this cloudy landscape.

2.

In the air wood-fire smoke
   as winter settles in for months to come.
Books are open, words are shared,
   the delicacy of crafting images,
      weighing the matter that matters,
         careful not to break an insight.

3.

I place three candles on the table,
   take three jellybeans from a jar.
I start the fire with a crossword,
   laughing that she has not finished
      this inchoate riddle of language.
         Just like this.

The Bird Call

in the Blue Mountains

A bird call across the sun-basked valley,
   a single sound in this vastness
     of gumtrees in June.
From this lookout we seek
   the source of the song,
     but a tapestry of treetops
      shelters it.
Again and again the bird calls,
   a limpid signal that life
     was given to this distant land.

We peer into the wilderness of green,
   now hallowed by
     a single bird, a single song.

The Golden Mile

Here is a road named The Golden Mile,
    golden for real estate, golden for gardens.
But now, this April, its true colours show,
    as Japanese maples, elms and some oaks,
        shower the street with their russet foliage.

We walk down the road in this amber glow,
    pausing to pick up a leaf here and there.
Here is a maple leaf, full of its beauty,
    palmately lobed, with five acute points.
Each leaf is subtly, discreetly serrated,
    and easily placed on the palm of the hand.
It glows with appeal, underrated perfection.
One leaf sought out, one leaf among many,
    a cascade of colour, autumnal chorus –
        a fitting tribute to a gifted maker.

Fire on the Mountain

I wake to the sound of an oscillating fan,
   the darkness like a shroud in our bedroom.
It is after midnight.
Earlier we walked to the top of the drive
     to watch the distant ridges glow with fire,
       the Grose Valley silent, waiting.
Lying here, I can smell the smoke seeping
   in through the window frames,
     although the house is shut against it.
My throat is dry, my pulse has quickened,
   some things are beyond my control.
I am like a wineskin in the smoke,
   parched by the threat of fire,
     stilled by this elemental rage.

A Handful of Quietness

from Ecclesiastes 4:6

A handful of quietness is this evening's gift.
Turning away from the winds that enchant,
   that rattle the frames and sing
      like sirens on the highway.
I invest in these still moments,
   carefully spreading silence on my face,
      on my hands, on my tired legs.
A handful of quietness goes a long way.
From this window I can see the moon,
   in masterful solitude,
      with dark clouds lingering.

My thoughts turn inward,
   away from the winds
      that fluster the leaves beneath the elm.

Peace.

The damp soil urges fungi,
   sasanqua petals fall.

The Lone Wolf

Rapacious God, devouring me with love,
  like a lone wolf howling at my door,
    knocking, scratching, pleading,
      as the storm winds buffet my living room.
I am alone with you without,
  for without you I am caught within
    a place where longing cries
      to turn the latch, for you to feed
        my hungry heart with bread and wine.

The wolf and lamb together are divine.

Bird life

Learning to look requires learning how to overlook
– James K. A. Smith

At breakfast I read your words of wisdom.

I will try to focus on a word, a bird, a person's deepest needs.
I will shut out the cymbals around me;
  a tumbler of pure insight will satisfy.

Through the window I can see
    a pair of King parrots
      feeding silently on lavender in the morning mist,
        in a gesture of demure sovereignty.

I do not need to see beyond this garden.

Lamplight

Dark corners gently lit by nuanced gestures.
Moonlight on venetian blinds
   and the soft sound of an owl at midnight.
A presence in the stillness.
Each night I hear his call, his comfort,
   exotic in suburbia, the pulse of otherness.
Over and over, his pianissimo tones
   steal into my thoughts, my dreams.
Somewhere in the darkened trees
   this sentinel, calm, alert, composed,
     soothes me with his steadiness.
Backlit by lunar lampshade clouds,
   he is ready to swoop and defend my prayers.

Crown of Thorns

The gardener, with gloved hands,
   carefully bundles pruned rose branches
      into the council bin.
Yesterday, the startling pain of a single thorn
   forced him inside for thick gloves.
He cannot imagine a crown of thorns.

Some think it was *Euphorbia milii*,
   its branches pliant with sharp, long thorns,
      disguised by bright green leaves and
         red bracts (like drops of blood) –
           a collusion of pain and beauty.

A crown of thorns for a youthful brow,
   blood trickling down a man's hair line,
      soaking the scalp, locks wet and clinging.
Andrea Solario captures that walk,
   the pallid brow, the downcast eyes,
      carrying the cross
         and a headband of needle-sharp hatred.

Where now the alabaster jar of soothing oil,
   the willingness to share his table?
Would I have tenderly lifted those akanthai
   from his suffering head, wiped the blood

from his suffering eyes, his darkened cheeks
and bandaged him in love, in care?

The gardener pauses from his work,
  looks upwards to the setting sun.
Across the trees a golden glow,
  like a crown of fire, a glory crown,
    and pain becomes a paean for
      this man of suffering, this man of sorrows.

The Waterman Pen

This pen writes good poetry.
Fashioned in blue, with embossed silver,
  it lifts the tone of my searching thoughts –
    it's the pride of my ink-filled armoury.
Like a confident boxer weighing in
  and poised to fight,
    it is ready for action, ready to write.
It is gracefully regal amongst its peers,
  a sublime companion for every page,
    cool to the touch, unflustered, firm,
      images crafted as pages turn.

A gift from my son,
  this jewel of simplicity,
    for those winter evenings
      in my quest for lucidity.

Metaphors

Metaphors live in the quietest places,
   under a leaf where fungi grows,
     in the trickle of dew on a windowpane,
       with the sigh from those darkening hills.
Demurring metaphors can blur
   the stark avidity of prose,
     blunting pomp and principles with
       texture and subtle timbre.
We hear them in unexpected spaces,
   alfresco tables, aperitif graces,
     unseen guests in every thread of words.
Like the smell of steak in passageways,
   they waft into our thinking,
     the gelatine in our gesturing,
       our conversational confidence.

Comfortable friends you can text any time,
   they are always there, ever ready,
     discreetly mellowing mundane moments,
       traces of poetry in each day's garments.
We are made for metaphors –
   without them, deficiency,
     brittle minds and porous thoughts,
     a bland, colourless canvas.
Poets sit in solitary rooms,
   capturing metaphors in jars,
     quietly releasing them into the wild
       to nurture the litter of language.

My Wife

I see your beauty in a smile,
   in silvered hair, in patterned blouse.
Like leaves tossed by a summer breeze,
    your laughter by this window, open,
      and footsteps down the well-worn slope,
        towards the house, towards the hearth
          of love, of warmth, of burnished comfort
            poured into every welcome cup of tea.
Shopping bags of gentleness are
   piled up in the living room –
    gifting my days, year after year,
     a balm for my unsteadiness.
Something lingers in these spaces,
   passed down to me in female graces,
    a glimpse, a gesture, eternal traces.

Incarnate God,
   I see your beauty in these places.

Resignation

On the park bench, Spring sunshine,
  a sparkling, high gloss invitation.
In this cleared space, open, verdant and empty,
  sheltered by tall gums, sighing,
    another voice whispered from the silence.

We sat there for some time,
  the sun on our faces,
    eyes downcast, silent, but hallowing.
A half hour passed, a waiting, a yearning,
  soothed by the stillness of this place.
Cradled in this midday moment,
  I surrendered all to a greater knowing.

Acknowledgements

Grateful acknowledgement is made to the editors of the following publications, in which some of the poems first appeared:

Hope Whispers, Poetica Christi Press, 2017, 'Perelandra' and 'Lamplight'.

Love's Footprint, Poetica Christi Press, 2019, 'Silence' and 'My Wife'.

CASE, New College, UNSW, 2021, and *Studio*, 2016, 'The Scholar.'

Studio, 2017, 'The Father's House', 2019, 'A Handful of Quietness', 2021, 'The Waterman Pen'.

Quadrant, 2021, 'Lent in the Blue Mountains' and 'The Lone Wolf'.

About The Author

Dr. Peter Stiles graduated from Macquarie University with a Bachelor of Arts and then a Master of Arts in English Literature. During those years he was pursuing a teaching career in NSW government primary schools (having graduated from Armidale Teachers College, where he won the Poetry Prize). In 1979 he transferred to teaching English in secondary schools, and subsequently became Head of English in two state high schools. He then undertook a Master of Education degree at the University of NSW.

After pursuing theological studies at Regent College, Vancouver, in 1987, he decided to undertake a Doctorate in Literature and Theology at the University of Glasgow. On his return from Glasgow, Peter chose to move into the private school sector, where he had executive roles at two leading private schools. Since 2016, Peter has been lecturing at Excelsia College, in Macquarie Park, for several years in the role of Senior Lecturer in Education.

Peter's collection of verse, *Trumped by Grace*, was shortlisted for The Australian Christian Book of the Year in 2017. His poetry has been published widely in Australia and the United States. He is currently engaged in editing a volume of poetry about the degradation of the natural environment.

www.ingramcontent.com/pod-product-compliance
Lightning Source LLC
Chambersburg PA
CBHW030303010526
44107CB00053B/1802